Favorite Recorder Tunes

Scottish Gems

Marcia Diehl

The Rottenburgh Baroque recorder model 4204 of boxwood on our cover is courtesy of Moeck Musikinstrumente + Verlag GmbH, Celle – Germany.

WWW.MELBAY.COM

Preface

The 41 *Scottish Gems* in this collection were arranged to fit within the comfortable range of both soprano and tenor recorders.

Music from this geographic area reflects the spirit of the land and its people. "Lick the Ladle, Sandy", "Dene Chased the Thief", "The Dandy Dancer", and "Rattlin' Roaring' Willie" are raucous tunes, which one can imagine dancers twirling into a dervish frenzy on a pocked wooden floor after a day of laboring on their precious farmland.

"Niel Gow's Lament", "Henry Martin", and "Gloomy Night" are melancholic songs expressing the darker side of the heart associated with the deep Celtic soul.

The lilting waltzes "Rosin the Bow", "The Rope Waltz", and "Leezie Lindsay Waltz" are elegant Scottish songs with a classical feel reminiscent of Mozart.

"The Kirrie Kebbuck" and "Bob Johnston" are examples of the Scottish dance form – the strathspey, featuring dotted rhythms, which provide the 'Scotch snaps'.

All countries have a repertoire of marches and the Celtic lands are no exception. "The Caledonian March" and "Gairsay March" are fine examples found in this collection.

"Annie Laurie" is a lovely, old Scottish song based on a poem said to have been written by William Douglas of Dumfriesshire in the 1700s, who was quite smitten with Annie Laurie. It's melody is familiar to many.

It is my utmost pleasure to present this compilation to you. I hope you enjoy it and that the tunes follow you throughout your day!

Marcia Diehl

Index

Caledonian March

Niel Gow's Lament

On a Bank of Flowers

Eppie Adair

♩ = 98
Em
Bm
Em
6
C
Em
Bm
12
D
Em
Am
B
Em
17
Bm
Em
22
C
Em

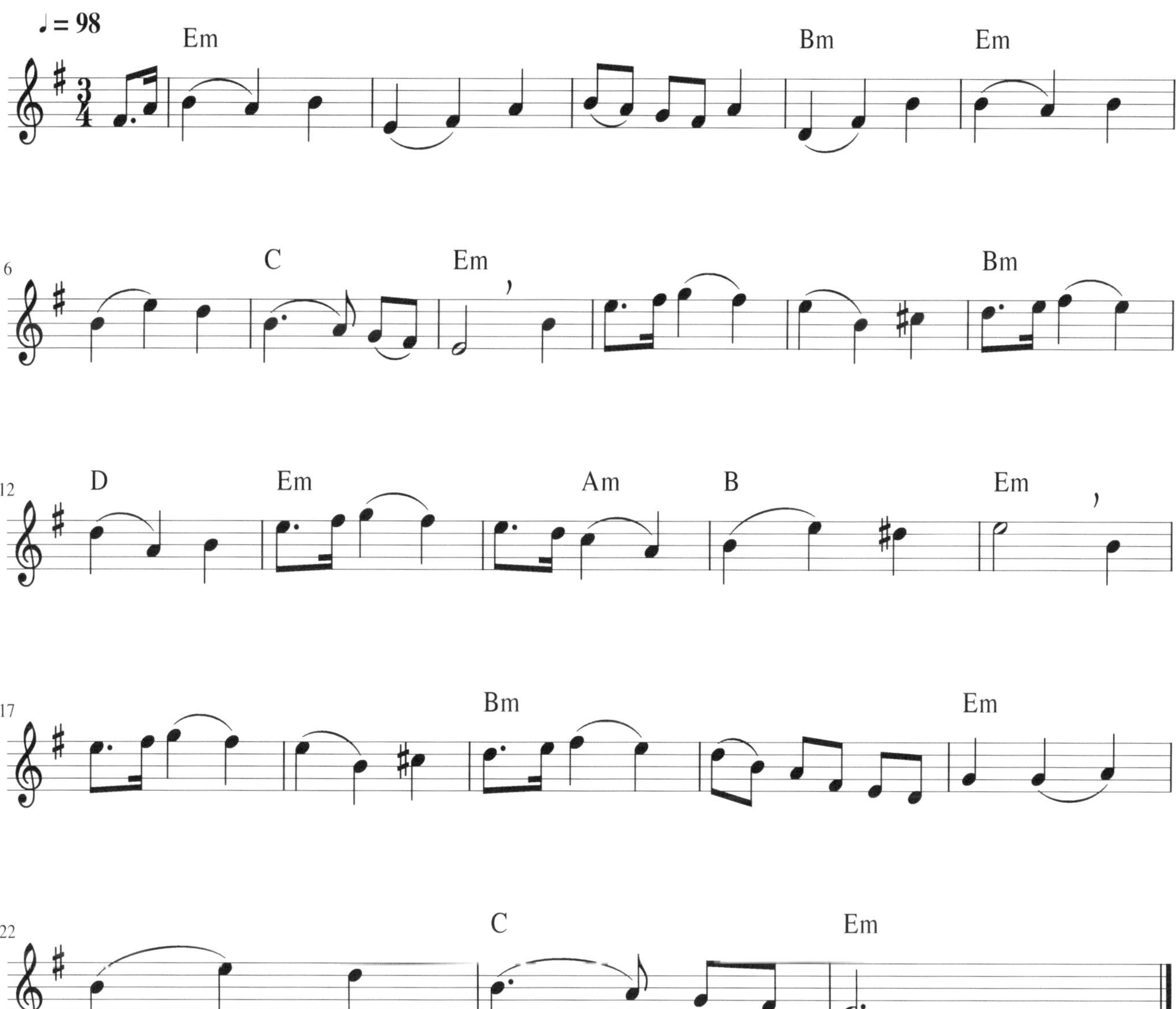

Lick the Ladle, Sandy

Pickle the Beats, Jeanne

for Steve and Jeanne

Marcia Diehl

G F G

6 F G Dm C

11 Am G F C

15 F Am Gsus4 G

19 F G

23 F G Dm C

27 Am G F C

31 F Am G

Annie Laurie

Henry Martin

Bob Johnston

The Rope Waltz

The Hills of Lorne

The Chevalier's Lament

Miss Shepherd

Dene Chased the Thief

Marcia Diehl

Catherine MacRitchie

Miss Catherine Maxwell's Scotch Measure

The Kirrie Kebbuck

Sweet Is the Lass that Dwells Among the Heather

Road to the Isles

If E'er Ye Do Well, It's a Wonder

Gan Ainm

♩ = 104
Am
G
Am
G
Em
5
Am
G
Am
G
Em
Am
9
G
Emn
13
A
G
Em
Am
17
G
Em
21
Am
G
Em
Am

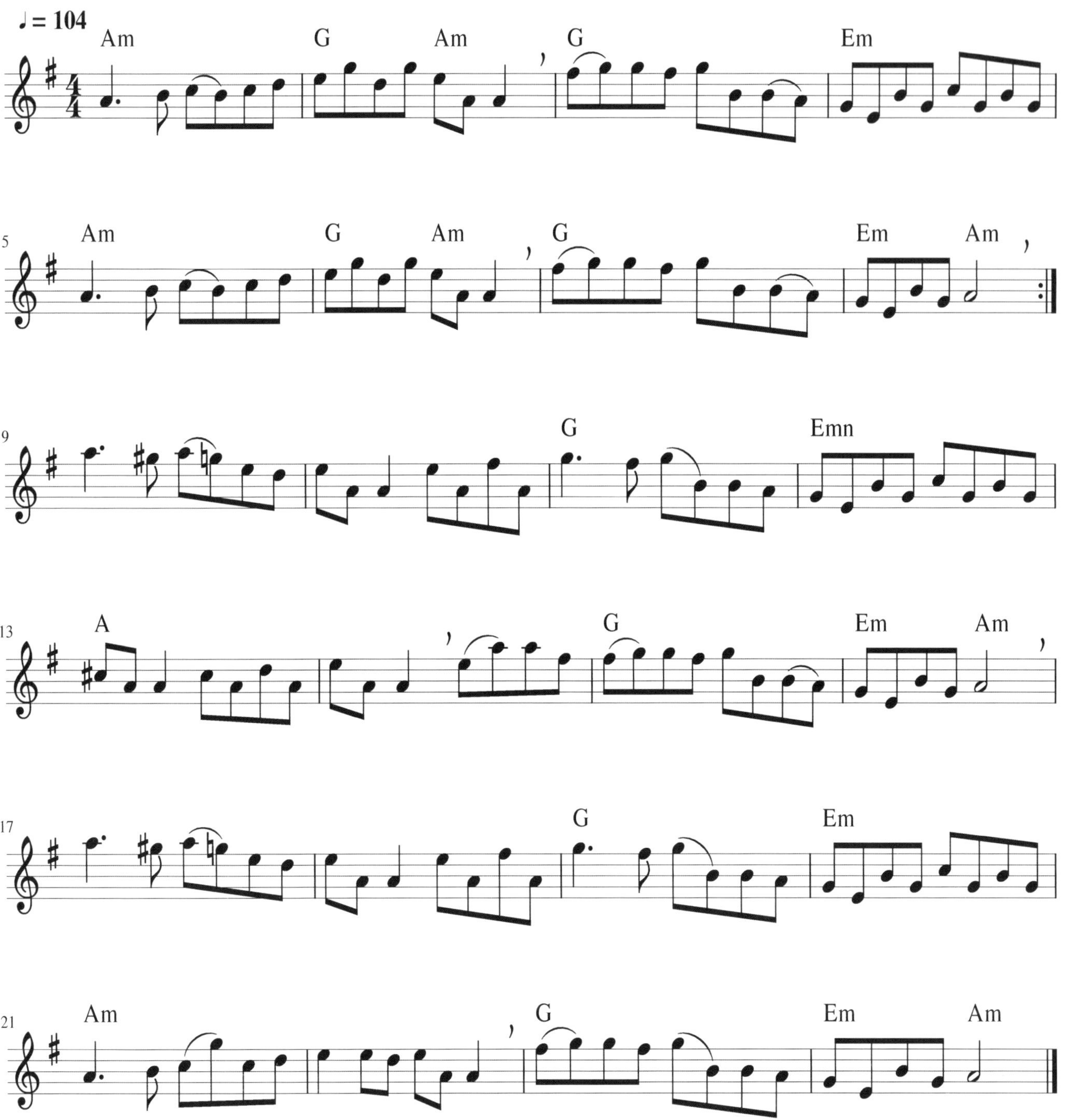

The Flowers of the Forest

MacPherson's Lament

The Dandy Dancer

The Braes of Lochiel

Leezie Lindsay Waltz

The Rights of Man

Stoneypath Tower

Rattlin' Roarin' Willie

Rosin the Bow

Kate Dalrymple

Highland Mary

Mairi's Wedding

Gloomy Night

My Love Is Like a Red Rose

Loch Tay Boat Song

Gairsay March

Dark Lochnagar

The Rowan Tree

The Flowers of Edinburgh

My Love She's But a Lassie Yet